VET

Animal Planet™

EMERGENCIES 24/7

Written by Susan Evento   Designed by On-Purpos, Inc.

Meredith® Books
Des Moines, Iowa

Marjorie Kaplan, President & General Manager, Animal Planet
Carol LeBlanc, Vice President, Licensing
Elizabeth Bakacs, Vice President, Creative Services
Brigid Ferraro, Director, Licensing
Caitlin Erb, Licensing Specialist

© 2007 Discovery Communications,
LLC. Animal Planet and the Animal
Planet logo are trademarks of Discovery
Communications, LLC, used under license.
All rights reserved.
www.animalplanet.com

Meredith Books
1716 Locust St.
Des Moines, IA 50309-3023
meredithbooks.com

Copyright © 2007 Meredith Corporation

First Edition.

All rights reserved.

Manufactured and printed in China.
ISBN: 978-0-696-23979-3 (tradepaper)
ISBN: 978-0-696-23810-9 (saddle-stitch)

We welcome your comments and suggestions.
Write to us at: Meredith Books, 1716 Locust St., Des Moines, IA 50309-302
Visit us at meredithbooks.com.

contents

24/7 Vet H

spital

Alameda East

Alameda East Veterinary Hospital's motto is "Your pets deserve our vets." For nearly 40 years, pets have been receiving the care they deserve from the dedicated vets at this high-tech hospital. Alameda East, located in Denver, Colorado is known throughout the country and the world for the advances it has made in veterinary science.

Every day of the year, every hour of the day, its doors are open to animals who need routine care and emergency care. The vets at Alameda East handle more than 10,000 cases a year! The highly trained staff provides a wide range of lifesaving measures to extremely sick and seriously injured animals.

Patients range from the usual domestic pets, such as dogs and cats, to more exotic animals, such as alligators and iguanas. No creature is too big or small. The vets at Alameda even make house calls to places like the Denver Zoo. They never know when they'll receive a call about a monkey that can't keep its food down or a hyena with a troublesome tumor. These vets need to be on their toes and ready to deal with some difficult and unusual cases!

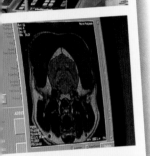

Come. Sit. Stay. Play at the Animal Lodge

In 2005, Alameda East opened Animal Lodge. Pet owners can take their pet there for a day at a time or for a longer stay, such as when they're on vacation. Any animal that is in day care or being boarded overnight has access to the vets at all times, day or night. Animals enjoy comfortable rooms with beds, windows, and even backyards. Some rooms have 24-hour webcams so anxious owners can watch their treasured pets at any time! Cats and dogs have designated playtimes and pool times. Dogs are also taken on leash walks.

Day care and boarding with lots of pampering aren't the only services the Animal Lodge has to offer. It also has a sports medicine and rehabilitation clinic. The vets and other specialists who work there develop programs for individual pets and work one-on-one with them. There are inground pools and underwater treadmills for water therapy. Water therapy allows pets to move their limbs while experiencing less stress on their joints. Swimming against a jet of water also increases animals' circulation and helps them regain a wider range of motion and flexibility. Electric stimulation and therapeutic workouts on exercise equipment also help animals grow stronger and healthier.

The specialists train working canines, including K-9 police dogs, search-and-rescue dogs, service dogs, and ranked show dogs.

Because obesity is becoming a more common problem among pets, Alameda East has a special scanner that measures body mass, including bone density and body fat.

The Animal Lodge also has a high-tech biomechanics laboratory. There they do advanced research to try to help lame dogs. They use digital motion to study dogs' movements.

Some of the specialists who work at the Animal Lodge use alternative medicine to help animals heal and get stronger. One of these is a Japanese therapy called Reiki. Therapists use their hands as a focus for healing and giving animals energy. Another alternative treatment used at Alameda is acupuncture, which involves the placement of needles in different parts of the body to heal it. Acupuncture is an ancient therapy that has been used on animals and people for thousands of years.

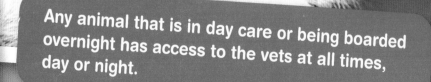

Any animal that is in day care or being boarded overnight has access to the vets at all times, day or night.

meet the vets

As a young child in Texas, Dr. Taylor befriended wild animals. When he was 14, he started working in a veterinary hospital.

Dr. Taylor: The Man who Started Emergency Vets

Dr. Robert Taylor started Alameda East in 1971 and realized, "If we were going to call ourselves a hospital, we needed to be open 24 hours a day."

Around-the-clock care was what pet owners needed, but the hours were often demanding on the small staff at Alameda East. Nearly 40 years and tens of thousands of operations later, Dr. Taylor has a much larger staff to run his hospital.

As a young child in Texas, Dr. Taylor befriended wild animals. When he was 14, he started working in a veterinary hospital. Before school, he cleaned cages and after school, he returned and often stayed for hours. "It just really captured my imagination," Dr. Taylor said.

Dr. Fitzgerald: A Funny Vet

Dr. Kevin Fitzgerald, also called "Fitz," took a long and uncommon path to becoming a vet. He didn't get into vet school the first time he tried, so he got a PhD instead. Then he taught school in Hawaii. During the summers, Dr. Fitzgerald worked as a bouncer (private security) for such famous musicians as The Rolling Stones, Willie Nelson, and Elvis Presley.

The next time Dr. Fitzgerald applied to vet school (eight years later), he was accepted. In 1983 he graduated from Colorado State University and in 1985 he became a vet at Alameda East. Dr. Fitzgerald has been working there for more than 20 years. During that time he has cared for thousands of domestic pets. He has also become one of Denver's leading exotic animal veterinarians.

Although Dr. Fitzgerald works long hours, he also has lots of fun making people laugh. For years he has done stand-up comedy. After a brief time performing in a tap-dancing group, Dr. Fitzgerald now taps to make people laugh.

Although Dr. Fitzgerald works long hours, he also has lots of fun making people laugh. For years he has done stand-up comedy.

Dr. Knor: A Born Vet

"I decided I was going to be a veterinarian when I was 5 years old," says Dr. Holly Knor. As a teenager, Dr. Knor worked for her family's vet, cleaning cages and answering the phone. Occasionally she was allowed to help care for an animal.

After graduating from vet school in 1995, Dr. Knor worked as an intern at Alameda East. A year later she became a member of the staff. Although Dr. Knor has been working there for many years, some of the cases still amaze her. "You'll get one that you think is so [unusual] that you'll never see anything like it again and boom! There is another one a year later."

Dr. Knor did not dream that her career as a vet would include being on television. She believes the show has given her an opportunity to teach pet owners how to better care for their pets.

As a teenager, Dr. Knor worked for her family's vet, cleaning cages and answering the phone.

Dr. Heather Hadley

+ **Worked for years as a veterinary assistant/ technician before going to vet school**

+ **Specialty interest: surgery**

meet the interns

Welcome to the world of interns at Alameda East. Workdays are often 16 hours long, and interns must work two months of overnight shifts. These new doctors deal with difficult cases on little sleep. That means they have to be prepared for the unexpected.

So why do these doctors intern at Alameda East? After graduating from veterinary school, some new doctors intern to help them determine which area of vet medicine they want to pursue. Many are drawn to Alameda's high-tech equipment, advanced research and procedures, and the dedicated doctors, like Dr. Taylor, Dr. Knor, and Dr. Fitzgerald, who mentor them.

These interns put in long hours because they love animals and get satisfaction from helping them through emergency situations. They know that interning at Alameda East means they will handle a variety of difficult cases that will challenge them to become better vets.

Dr. Michelle Nanfelt

+ **Worked as a veterinary/surgery technician before going to vet school**

+ **Specialty interest: surgery**

Dr. David Gall

+ **Formerly worked as a therapist for people**

+ **Specialty interest: radiology**

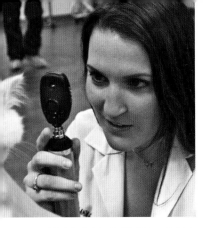

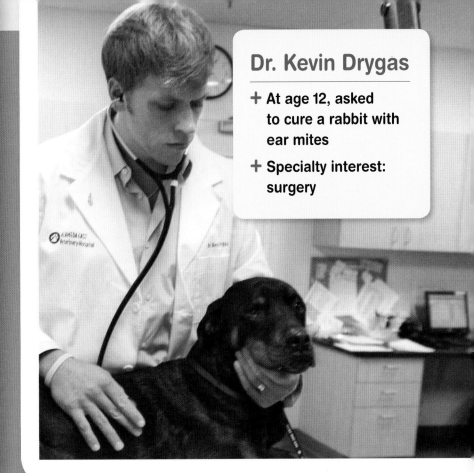

Dr. Kevin Drygas

+ At age 12, asked to cure a rabbit with ear mites
+ Specialty interest: surgery

Dr. Blair Willman

+ Grew up in a farming community with many animals; her family adopted strays
+ Specialty interests: dermatology, animal behavior, and exotics

Dr. Shana O'Marra

+ Worked part time as an emergency/ critical care veterinary technician while studying to become a vet
+ Specialty interests: emergency medicine and critical care

Dr. Erik Anderson

+ Worked at the Humane Society in his early teens; later worked as a veterinary assistant/technician
+ Specialty interests: anesthesiology, oncology, radiology, and internal medicine

Case Studie

Fractured

| EMERGENCY VET: | Dr. Jason Wheeler |
| PATIENT: | Cody, a blue heeler dog |

DIAGNOSIS: What happens when dogs fight? Well, the loser of the dogfight just might end up looking like Cody. Cody, a blue heeler, which is a type of Australian sheepdog, got on the wrong side of a fight with some rottweilers. His trachea is torn and he has air trapped in his chest. A bone in his leg, called the radius, is broken.

TREATMENT: Dr. Wheeler thinks Cody has a good chance of healing and behaving. However, Cody's owners cannot afford the surgery he needs. They are also afraid they won't be able to control his behavior with other dogs in the future. They make the difficult decision to give up Cody.

Dr. Wheeler promises the family that he will find Cody a good home. Cody receives an excellent home: Dr. Wheeler decides to adopt Cody!

FOLLOW-UP: Although Cody is healing nicely, it will take some time. Dr. Wheeler helps speed Cody's recovery by playing outside with him.

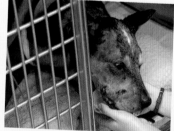

A Headache
That Won't Quit

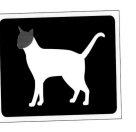 

EMERGENCY VET: Dr. Robert Taylor

PATIENT: Willy, a cat

DIAGNOSIS: Poor Willy was bitten by a dog when he was 3 months old. Two years later, he's still in pain. The dog bit into Willy's sinus cavity. The bite became infected and caused the sinus cavity to swell. The swelling keeps Willy's sinuses from draining through his nose, so he gets bad headaches. His owner, Stephanie, brings him to Alameda East.

Dr. Robert Taylor also has painful headaches, so Willy has an understanding vet.

TREATMENT: Dr. Taylor performs surgery on Willy's head. He needs to clean out the sinus cavity to prevent this from happening again.

Dr. Taylor stitches up the opening. Poor Willy's forehead looks like the lacing on a football. Frankenkitty!

FOLLOW-UP: When Willy wakes up from surgery, he is not happy. And of course, he doesn't look much better! But the next day his owner takes him home. The second day home Willy is already running and playing. Six weeks after his surgery, Willy no longer looks like Frankenkitty. His scars have healed and his headaches are gone!

ALBERT & SPIKE

An Alligator with a Taste For Hot Dogs

EMERGENCY VET:	Dr. Kevin Fitzgerald
PATIENT:	Albert, an alligator

DIAGNOSIS: Tim brings his alligator Albert to Alameda East after feeding him a hot dog. The hot dog made Albert bloated, so Tim wants him checked. Baby Albert weighs only 1 pound. He has a lot of growing to do to reach the 200 pounds he'll weigh in about five years. Like any other animal, he enjoys being petted and scratched behind the neck. He even enjoys walking on a leash. And like other pets he shouldn't be fed table scraps.

TREATMENT: Dr. Fitzgerald uses a syringe of medicine that will clean out his insides.

FOLLOW-UP: Albert's bloating is gone, and there won't be any more hot dogs in his diet!

A Moneymaking Iguana

EMERGENCY VETS:	Dr. Kevin Fitzgerald & Dr. Robert Taylor
PATIENT:	Spike, an iguana

DIAGNOSIS: Spike was vomiting a lot the night before. Spike's owner Ann thinks her iguana climbed onto the kitchen counter and ate some dry cat food.

Dr. Fitzgerald takes X-rays, but not easily! Spike is one feisty iguana with a powerful tail. Iguanas are territorial and Spike is no exception. Spike and Dr. Fitzgerald have a brief wrestling match; Dr. Fitzgerald wins.

TREATMENT: The X-rays show Spike ate several coins. New pennies have zinc, which is toxic, so this worries the owner and the vets. Dr. Fitzgerald and Dr. Taylor operate on Spike to remove two dimes and five pennies. They were corroded, which means that they have been inside Spike for a while. The toxic coins were making Spike sick.

FOLLOW-UP: Twenty-four hours after surgery the spirited iguana is giving the doctors a run for their money. He wants his 25 cents back. Spike must be feeling better because he wants to wrestle.

Spike's owner now has change for a phone call and her iguana is on the road to recovery.

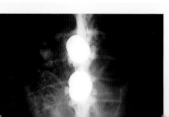

A Troublesome Tumor

EMERGENCY VETS: Dr. Dan Steinheimer & Dr. Robert Taylor

PATIENT: Bear, a spotted hyena

DIAGNOSIS: There's a spotted hyena at the Denver Zoo named Bear—go figure! Veterinarians at the zoo discover a tumor in Bear's stomach. To help them find out more about it, the zoo calls in vets from Alameda East. Alameda's Dr. Steinheimer gives Bear an ultrasound. He finds a tumor about the size of a tennis ball. Although it is near important organs, he thinks they may be able to operate on Bear and remove it.

TREATMENT: The next step is to take a biopsy of the tumor to find out whether it is cancerous. A biopsy is a procedure during which a small sample of tissue, cells, or fluids is removed for a closer examination. Dr. Taylor takes out a piece of the tumor. Although it tests positive for cancer, it is all in one place. Dr. Taylor removes the tumor.

FOLLOW-UP: Bear will be spotted at the zoo for many years to come!

BEAR

Ernie Swallowed Antifreeze

EMERGENCY VETS: Doctors on staff	
PATIENT: Ernie, a Labrador retriever	

DIAGNOSIS: Brian, Ernie's owner, was draining his truck's radiator in his garage. In a flash, while Brian's back was turned, his 2-year-old black Lab lapped some drained fluid containing antifreeze. Antifreeze is sweet, and dogs like its taste, but even a small amount can kill them. Ernie's lucky, because his owner brings him in quickly, and most of what he drank is still in his stomach and hasn't been absorbed into his bloodstream.

TREATMENT: First, the vets make Ernie vomit. Then they try to give him charcoal, which will absorb the toxin to make doubly sure it doesn't get into his system. But Ernie refuses to cooperate, and they finally decide that administering the charcoal is not worth the price the dog is paying in stress and possible harm.

The charcoal was just an added measure to protect Ernie. It's more important to give Ernie the antidote, which will prevent any remaining antifreeze from breaking down into its toxic elements in his system. Along with the antidote, the vets give Ernie fluids. They keep him for two days so they can check his kidneys to make sure they aren't damaged.

FOLLOW-UP: Two days later Ernie is ready to go home. Ernie's constant howling is a good sign that he is healthy. His blood tests show no sign of damage.

Antifreeze is sweet, and dogs like its taste, but even a small amount can kill them.

A Therapy Tabby

EMERGENCY VETS: Dr. Holly Knor & Dr. Robert Taylor	
PATIENT: Thomas, a tabby cat	

DIAGNOSIS: Officer Lopez received a call about an accident. When he arrived at the scene, he followed paw marks into the snow on the side of the road. A cat had been hit by a car and flew over a fence into a cemetery. Officer Lopez found the cat under a bush and brought him to Alameda East.

TREATMENT: Although the snow helped the officer locate Thomas, being in the snow for some time caused Thomas's body temperature to drop well below normal. A vet technician dries the cat's fur with a hair dryer to help raise his temperature. As Thomas' temperature rises, the staff at Alameda tries to locate his owner so they can take X-rays. A collar with tags helps Alameda find this tabby's home: Thomas lives at a retirement home where he is a therapy cat.

The vets at Alameda take X-rays that show two fractures to the cat's pelvis. If not fixed, Thomas won't be able to walk again. The fractures are in a small area and are difficult for Dr. Taylor to reach. In less than 20 minutes, Dr. Taylor has successfully placed a pin and a screw connecting the tabby's pelvis.

FOLLOW-UP: Two days after surgery, Thomas is ready to return to the retirement home. Residents there will help nurse Thomas back to health just as he has helped them become healthier.

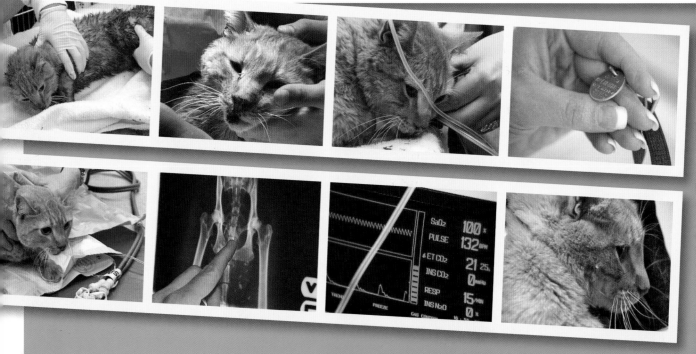

Shrinking Samson

EMERGENCY VETS: Dr. Doug Santen & Dr. Robert Taylor

PATIENT: Samson, a rottweiler

DIAGNOSIS: Samson, a 5-year-old rottweiler, is losing weight. The once-healthy dog weighed 105 pounds. He has lost 35 pounds and now weighs 70 pounds! His owners Dean and Margaret take Samson to Alameda East to find out why their pet is shrinking. Dr. Santen uses an ultrascan and finds that Samson has a tumor in his stomach. Dr. Santen thinks they can successfully remove the tumor. The anxious owners want to go ahead with the operation. "This dog smells flowers," says Dean. "He sticks his nose in tulips as he walks down the street."

TREATMENT: When Dr. Santen and Dr. Taylor perform surgery on Samson, they find a tumor the size of a small watermelon. It has destroyed his left kidney. Dr. Taylor removes the large tumor but finds that the cancer has spread throughout Samson's body. The vets discover that it is a type of cancer that can't be treated.

FOLLOW-UP: Dean and Margaret take Samson home and make the most of every day they have together. Samson still enjoys running and playing with the family's other two rottweilers and the neighbors' dogs.

A Relationship
Stretched Thir

| EMERGENCY VET: **Dr. Holly Knor** |
| PATIENT: **Duchess, a German shepherd** |

DIAGNOSIS: Duchess, a 12-year-old German shepherd, has a rubber band stretched around her neck. It has probably been there for a week. The pressure of the rubber band around the neck has caused it to cut into the skin; the skin has become infected.

Owner Carol couldn't see the rubber band, but she could smell a bad odor. She thought the smell was caused by one of Duchess' constant ear infections. But as Carol looked closer, she saw Duchess had a rubber band around her neck. Carol clipped the band but couldn't get it out of her dog's fur and skin. She brought Duchess to Alameda East.

TREATMENT: Dr. Holly Knor removes the rubber band and cleans the area. She puts a bandage on the wound and prescribes antibiotics to clear up the infection.

FOLLOW-UP: After a week Duchess' wounds are healing well, and Carol's daughter has learned an important lesson about caring for her dog.

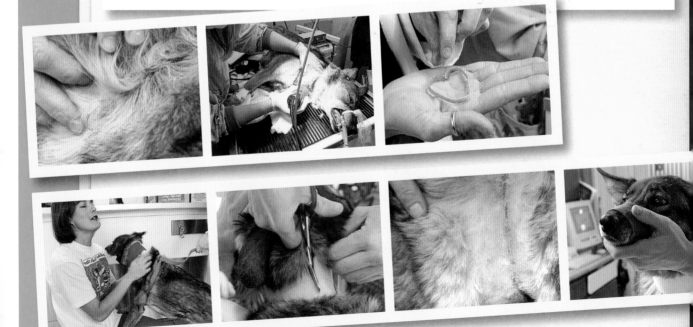

The Naked Truth

EMERGENCY VET:	Dr. Kevin Fitzgerald
PATIENT:	Mr. Fancy Pants, a Devon rex kitten

DIAGNOSIS: Mr. Fancy Pants, a Devon rex kitten, was taken home by his new owner Sarah one week ago. This kitten's temporary baldness (caused by natural shedding) uncovers ringworm.

Ringworm is a common infection. From its name, you'd think that a worm causes it, but it's actually caused by a fungus. The fungus is highly contagious and can be passed from animals to humans. His new owner has ringworm too!

Dr. Fitzgerald shines an ultraviolet light on the kitten's ringworm. The fungus on the kitten's skin glows bright green.

TREATMENT: This kitten has several baths in his future. (And like most cats, Mr. Fancy Pants isn't a fan of water!) Each bath will be accompanied by an application of lime sulfur on the cat's skin. The water and medicated shampoo as well as the lime sulfur will kill the fungus.

FOLLOW-UP: His ringworm should be gone before his adult coat grows in. Both the pet and owner should be fungus-free by then too.

A Hairy Operation

EMERGENCY VETS:	Dr. Kevin Fitzgerald & Dr. Robert Taylor
PATIENT:	Freckles, a rabbit

DIAGNOSIS: Monika was up all night, rubbing her rabbit's tummy. She saw Freckles eat some pieces of a towel and believes that is what is upsetting her rabbit's stomach. Freckles hasn't been able to get rid of waste in a while and is clearly uncomfortable.

TREATMENT: Dr. Fitzgerald and Dr. Taylor discuss the options for treating Freckles. Dr. Fitzgerald thinks a hairball is the problem. Unfortunately the mass is so large, they need to operate. Rabbits get stressed easily, so the vets must be sure to use just the right amount of anesthesia to put Freckles under while they operate. Dr. Taylor performs surgery on the rabbit and finds a large hairball, as Dr. Fitzgerald suspected. They remove the mass of hair and check the large intestine for any other damage. Part of the bowel is bruised, but other than that, it looks OK.

FOLLOW-UP: Freckles will need some fluids while waking up. The bruise will heal, and after some rest, Freckles will be as good as new!

An Itch that Needs to Be Scratched

EMERGENCY VET: **Dr. David Panciera**
PATIENT: **Ben, a golden retriever**

DIAGNOSIS: Ben is a therapy dog. He lives and works at a center where people who have suffered illnesses are going through therapy. Ben's job is to befriend the patients and encourage them to feel better.

He has helped one patient, Jim, walk again. When Jim came to live at the center he was in a wheelchair. While Jim progressed from a wheelchair and walker to walking unaided, Ben was there every step of the way. Ben provided love and physically helped Jim keep his balance while relearning to walk. "He's such a partner. He's just part of my life now. Good friend. He's a very good friend," says Jim.

But these days Ben is not feeling well. When Ben doesn't feel well, no one at the center feels great. Ben has been spending most of his time on the floor, scratching his tummy, feet, and face. And Ben hasn't been eating. Like many golden retrievers, Ben suffers from allergies. People who suffer from allergies often have runny eyes and sneeze a lot; dogs get itchy skin. Ben had been taking medicine for his allergies, but it wasn't something that should be taken over long periods of time.

TREATMENT: Dr. Panciera finds that Ben's constant scratching has broken the skin in places and caused an infection. The vet gives Ben antibiotics to clear up the infection and sends him back to the center. In the meantime Dr. Panciera starts to work on a long-term treatment plan to help Ben's allergies.

FOLLOW-UP: Back at the center, many patients, including Jim, are ready to provide Ben with the love and care he needs to feel better.

BEN

Dose of the
Wrong Medicine

EMERGENCY VET: Dr. Laura Peycke	
PATIENTS: Dakota and Aspen, dogs	

DIAGNOSIS: Sharon drove home at lunchtime to see her dog Dakota, a golden retriever. And it's a good thing she did! Dakota and Aspen, her roommate Anne's dog, raided the bathroom. They got into everything—lipstick, makeup, and medicine, such as ibuprofen. Sharon has no way of knowing which dog ate what.

Dakota looks OK, maybe just a bit guilty; but Sharon can't wake Aspen, a black lab. During the five-minute drive to Alameda, she pulls Aspen's tail and nudges him, but he won't stir.

TREATMENT: Dr. Peycke is most concerned about the ibuprofen. Even in tiny amounts, this drug can cause kidney damage in dogs. She begins by emptying both dogs' stomachs. It doesn't look as if Dakota has eaten any of the ibuprofen, but Aspen ate a lot—even part of the plastic bottle!

The next step is giving the dogs liquid charcoal directly to their stomachs, where it will absorb any toxins that remain. The charcoal will soon pass through the dogs' systems, carrying the toxins with it.

FOLLOW-UP: The next morning, the dogs are eating, drinking, and urinating. Urination is the best sign that their kidneys are not damaged. Sharon and Anne have learned their lesson. From now on, they will lock up everything in their bathroom.

A Shocking Story

EMERGENCY VET: **Dr. Kevin Fitzgerald**
PATIENT: **Robinson, a ferret**

DIAGNOSIS: Robinson, a healthy 1-year-old ferret, got a routine shot. On the way home from the vet, he became still and limp. His owners immediately brought him to Alameda East. Apparently the little ferret was allergic to the shot and had gone into shock.

TREATMENT: Dr. Fitzgerald gives Robinson a shot of epinephrine to stabilize the ferret's heart. Then he puts him in a cage with oxygen. Slowly Robinson is weaned off the oxygen.

FOLLOW-UP: At first he is wobbly, but soon he is back to his normal, active self. Later that day Robinson goes home with his owners.

Hamster Help

EMERGENCY VET: **Dr. Kevin Fitzgerald**
PATIENT: **Juliet, a Syrian dwarf hamster**

DIAGNOSIS: Juliet is a Syrian dwarf hamster who was abused by her former owner. Her new owner Doris is training her "that the hand is loving." But Doris wears a glove when handling Juliet in case Juliet doesn't get the message and tries to bite. While petting her hamster, she discovered a strange spot on the 11-month-old's ear. She ran a cotton swab under warm water, held it to the spot, and out came blood.

TREATMENT: Dr. Fitzgerald discovers that Juliet has a tiny tumor in her ear; he takes a biopsy of the tumor. A biopsy is a procedure during which a small sample of tissue, cells, or fluids is removed for a closer examination.

FOLLOW-UP: Two days later, Juliet is eating well, which is a good sign. The results come back on the biopsy, and she is cancer-free. Her owner is delighted. Doris must give her medicine every day and call Dr. Fitzgerald to report on Juliet's progress.

For Pete's Sake

EMERGENCY VET:	Dr. Kevin Fitzgerald
PATIENT:	Pete, a turtle

DIAGNOSIS: "I always wanted a turtle," says Clayton, "and now I have one!" The lucky 5-year-old came upon a box turtle he named Pete. But Clayton and his mother notice that Pete has a hole in his shell. Mother and son bring Pete to Alameda East.

TREATMENT: Dr. Fitzgerald discovers that Pete has been shot with a pellet gun. He uses a material called fiberglass to cover the hole.

FOLLOW-UP: As Pete grows his shell will heal and push off the patch. Then he'll be whole again!

A Python with a Stuffy Nose

EMERGENCY VET:	Dr. Kevin Fitzgerald
PATIENT:	Pet-store python

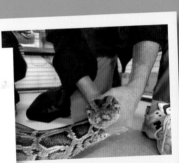

DIAGNOSIS: Dr. Fitzgerald makes a house call to a pet store that sells snakes. The owner has noticed that his 11-foot 2-inch python has a stuffy nose. She has been quiet, tired, and making a loud gurgling noise.

Dr. Fitzgerald knows that with a stuffed nose, this reptile, which relies on its sense of smell, won't be able to detect her prey. Without eating, she will grow weak and likely catch pneumonia. The poor python is trying hard to clear her nose.

TREATMENT: Dr. Fitzgerald puts her on an antibiotic and instructs the owners to give the python a dose each day for a week.

FOLLOW-UP: A week later the perky python is healthy and ready to go to a new home.

Xena, Warrior Kitty

EMERGENCY VET: Dr. Jeff Steen

PATIENT: Xena, a cat

DIAGNOSIS: Xena, a 3-year-old cat, has certainly earned her name. She's one feisty critter. "She bounces off walls … and she's just fun," says her owner Kathrine. One day while Kathrine was using paint stripper on her stairway, Xena jumped in the middle of her work and became covered in the toxic gel.

TREATMENT: Quick-thinking Kathrine immediately put Xena in the bathtub and washed her. The paint stripper badly burned Xena, who started howling loudly.

Kathrine brings Xena to the vets at Alameda East Veterinary Hospital. She isn't sure whether Xena has licked herself and perhaps swallowed some of the gel.

Dr. Steen looks inside Xena's mouth and doesn't find any blisters. That's good news. He tells Kathrine that she did the right thing by washing off Xena.

FOLLOW-UP: Kathrine watches Xena closely to make sure she doesn't have any problems. Before long the feisty cat is bouncing off walls and is up to her old tricks!

A Game of Fetch Gone Wrong

EMERGENCY VETS: Dr. Kevin Fitzgerald & Dr. Robert Taylor
PATIENT: Rocky, a golden retriever

DIAGNOSIS: Owner Melissa is playing fetch with her energetic 5-year-old retriever when suddenly the stick disappears. Rocky sits down, paws at his throat, and starts to gag. Melissa rushes him to Alameda.

Dr. Fitzgerald can't see the stick, but he can see many cuts inside the dog's mouth. He takes X-rays that show the stick is lodged in Rocky's throat. It's a larger stick than he expected—9 inches long! Dr. Fitzgerald is afraid the stick has also cut the inside of Rocky's throat and esophagus, a tube that runs from his throat to his chest.

TREATMENT: The stick is so long Dr. Taylor needs to cut it in half, before he can remove it surgically. It's a difficult procedure to extract the stick without doing harm to Rocky's important organs. The good news is the stick has not cut the esophagus. The only wound is at the back of the mouth where the stick hit when it first entered Rocky's mouth. Although this was an unusual accident to have happened, the results couldn't be better.

FOLLOW-UP: Three days after the accident, Rocky is ready to fetch again. But no more sticks for Rocky! Now Melissa throws large, soft fetch toys that Rocky can't possibly swallow.

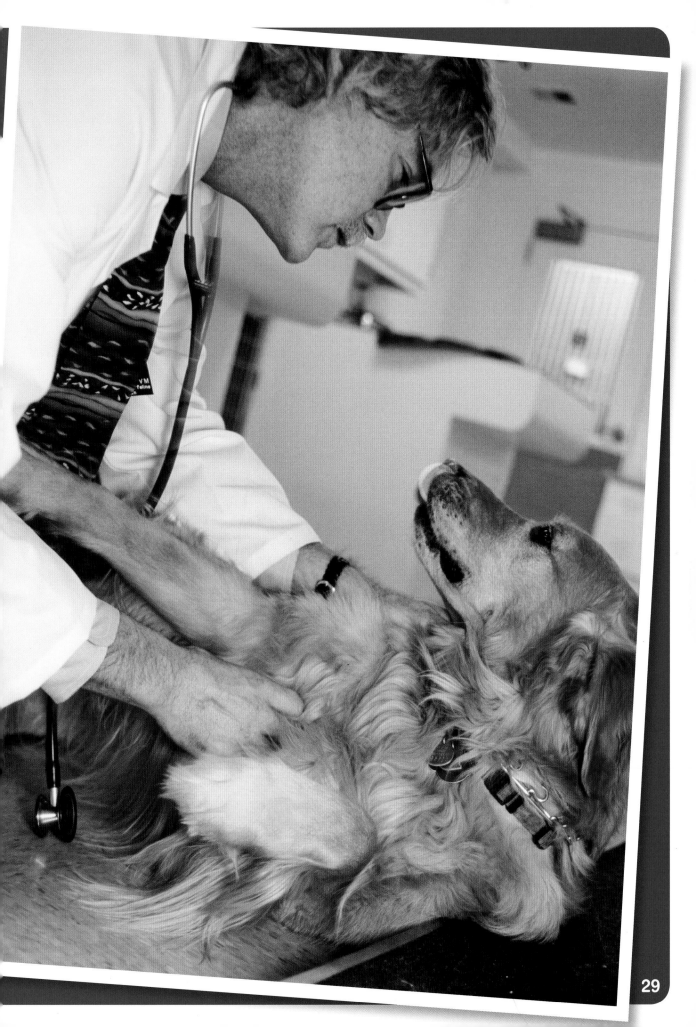

Open Wide, Priscilla

EMERGENCY VET: Dr. Andy Hofeling

PATIENT: Priscilla, a hedgehog

DIAGNOSIS: Priscilla's owner Tricia worries that her 3-month-old hedgehog isn't eating. As she examines her pet, Tricia finds what she believes to be a sore on the roof of Priscilla's mouth. Hedgehogs are known for getting cancer, so Tricia fears the worst.

TREATMENT: Dr. Hofeling opens Priscilla's mouth and to his surprise he finds this hedgehog has a taste for peanuts! One is stuck to the roof of Priscilla's mouth. Dr. Hofeling removes the peanut and the lucky hedgehog is on her way home.

FOLLOW-UP: Priscilla's relieved owner takes her home and promises the vet her hedgehog will have a peanut-free diet.

A Sewing Cat

EMERGENCY VETS: Dr. Katie Miller & Dr. Amy Estrada

PATIENT: Katrina, a cat

DIAGNOSIS: Lynne, Katrina's owner, left her sewing basket open. Curious Katrina, an 11-year-old cat, soon started throwing up. Thread was dangling from her mouth, and Lynne pulled the rest of it out. Since that time Katrina has been sluggish and vomiting clear liquid. Lynne brings her to Alameda because she fears Katrina has swallowed a needle as well.

TREATMENT: Dr. Miller examines Katrina's mouth and finds a needle stuck in the back of her throat. Dr. Estrada and Dr. Miller remove the needle carefully. Success! The roof of Katrina's mouth looks fine; no damage was done.

FOLLOW-UP: Lynne takes Katrina home and keeps her sewing basket closed and out of sight.

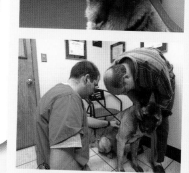

Round TWO!

| EMERGENCY VET: | Dr. Corey Wall |
| PATIENT: | Bailey, an Akita |

DIAGNOSIS: Bailey, an Akita, is at Alameda East with a bleeding mouth. He picked a fight with another dog over food—and lost. But the fight isn't out of Bailey yet. Fortunately, Dr. Corey Wall is ready. Even so, he ends up on the floor, wrestling Bailey to give him an injection that will calm him down. The doctor attributes his ability to control the feisty dog to his training in martial arts.

TREATMENT: Dr. Wall finds several wounds inside Bailey's mouth that need to be stitched. He uses stitches that will eventually dissolve. This way neither he nor Bailey will have to go another round on the floor at Alameda East!

FOLLOW-UP: Bailey will heal nicely.

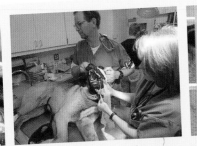

A Monkey Can't Keep Her Food Down

EMERGENCY VET: **Dr. Doug Santen**
PATIENT: **Gerta, a red-capped monkey**

DIAGNOSIS: Dr. Doug Santen visits the Primate House at the Denver Zoo. Dr. Felicia Knightly is the zoo's vet, but she has called Dr. Santen to help her figure out what is wrong with Gerta, a 16-year-old red-capped monkey. Gerta vomits after she eats. Dr. Knightly thinks it might be a social problem within the monkey society at the zoo that is upsetting Gerta.

Dr. Santen uses an endoscope, a long tube with a camera attached, to look inside Gerta. He decides to biopsy Gerta's digestive tract. A biopsy is a procedure during which a small sample of tissue, cells, or fluids is removed for a closer examination. Gerta's tissue samples are removed by placing a small grabber through the endoscope. Dr. Santen takes several samples. He thinks everything looks good, but the results of the biopsies will tell the full story. The results show that Gerta has gastritis. Dr. Knightly's prediction was correct. Gerta has been experiencing stress, which causes her to produce more stomach acid. Too much stomach acid causes gastritis, which results in an infection that causes vomiting.

TREATMENT: The primate keeper will give Gerta two liquid antibiotics on bread with peanut butter and a little bit of honey. Gerta has a sweet tooth, and all the sweet stuff will disguise the taste of the medicine.

FOLLOW-UP: Gerta is eating well and keeping her food down. The monkeys also seem to be getting along better.

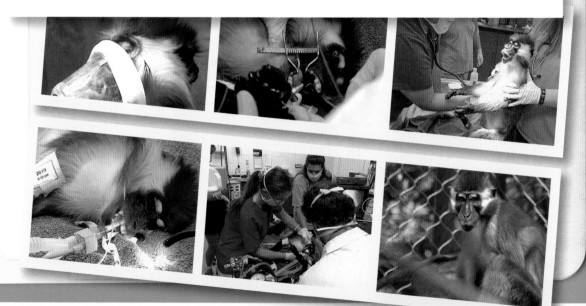

GERTA

Unwanted Visitor

EMERGENCY VETS: Dr. Robert Taylor & Dr. Jason Wheeler

PATIENT: Scooby, a schnauzer mix

DIAGNOSIS: Carol awoke one morning and found her dog Scooby unable to get out of his bed. He was listless and he was crying.

Just the week before, Scooby was scampering through the mountains with owners Dick and Carol. Even though the owners checked him for ticks upon their return from the mountains, the vets at Alameda find a strange-looking tick on Scooby's throat. Ticks carry toxins, or poisons, that can affect nerves and muscles and cause paralysis.

TREATMENT: The vets give Scooby a bath in a solution that will kill any other ticks that might have hitched a ride home with him. Scooby stays at Alameda while he deals with getting rid of the toxins in his system. The next day, although somewhat shaky, the little schnauzer is walking around. Usually paralysis from a tick takes longer to go away, but luckily this tick's toxin isn't as powerful.

FOLLOW-UP: The owners take Scooby home and will be more careful to check their dog for unwanted visitors.

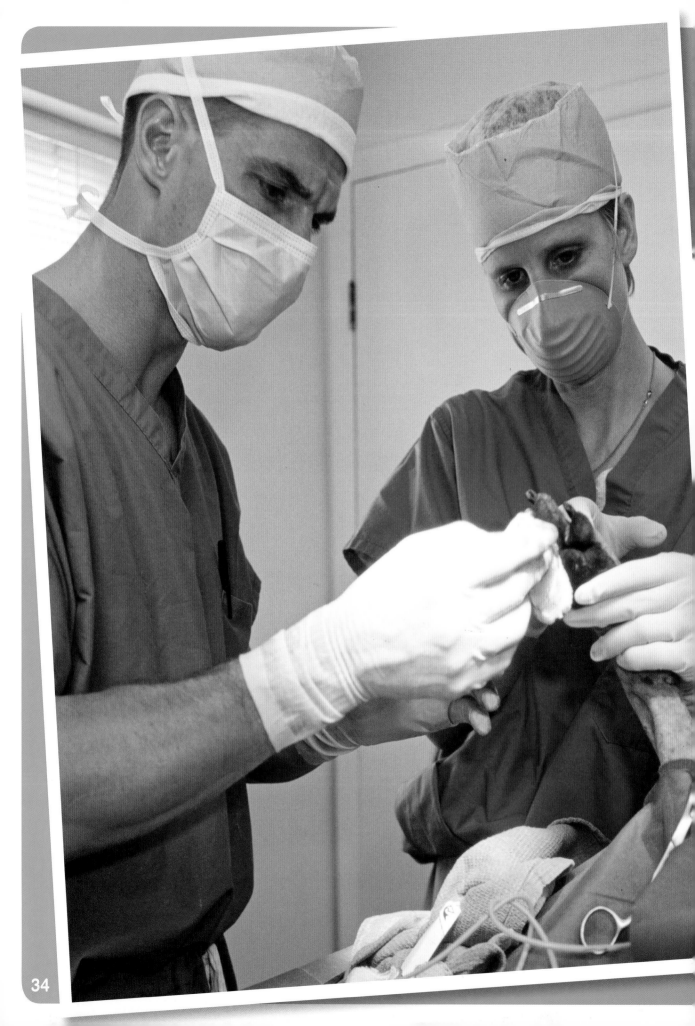

A Dog Born to Run

EMERGENCY VET: Dr. Robert Taylor	
PATIENT: Nick, a Aussie shepherd mix	

DIAGNOSIS: Nick is missing the middle pad on one of his front paws. Nick puts a lot of weight on his front legs and paws as he moves about. Without a pad replacement, Nick won't be able to walk well and certainly will not be able to run. Nick has been owner Kim's running buddy. She's hoping that Nick will be able to run with her again after the vets at Alameda treat him.

TREATMENT: Dr. Robert Taylor has a two-step plan for helping Nick. In the first step he plans to remove the bone on the outside of Nick's paw and then wait a week to let the skin heal.

In step two the following week, Dr. Taylor removes Nick's outer paw pad (where he removed the bone) and places it in the center of his paw. Although this side pad is smaller than the center pad, it will grow nearly double in size to fill the space! Dr. Taylor places a bulky bandage on Nick's paw to keep him from trying to move around. Nick must stay off this paw for a couple of weeks to let it heal.

FOLLOW-UP: Unfortunately, eight days after surgery, Nick somehow gets out of the house and tries to follow his owner on a run. In his effort to join Kim, Nick untangles the bandage and pulls a few of the stitches loose. He goes back to Alameda East for a third surgery to repair the damage. This time Dr. Taylor wraps Nick's paw with his leg bent so he won't be able to put his paw down.

The pad is growing and the site is healing. Within a month or so Nick will be able to run on the grass with Kim!

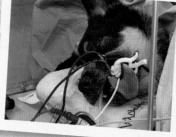

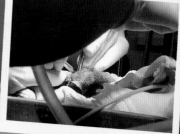
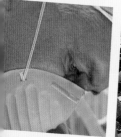
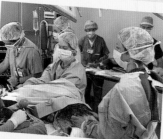

An Unexpected Emergency

EMERGENCY VET: Dr. John Fiddler

PATIENT: Shadow, a lab

DIAGNOSIS: Joe and John and their father Jim, are paramedics. They are used to handling human medical emergencies. When their lab Shadow is hit by a car, they leave his care to the vets at Alameda East.

Shadow has a broken shoulder blade. He also has blood in his urine. That is a sign that his bladder might have burst. They must wait until the next morning to find out whether Shadow will pull through.

TREATMENT: "When something like this happens," says Jim, "we always come together." The dog's family waits overnight. The next morning Shadow's condition is much improved.

FOLLOW-UP: His urine is clear of blood and his shoulder will heal on its own. The men in the family return to the kind of emergencies they are best prepared to handle.

Peetie's Unusual Diet

EMERGENCY VET: Dr. Jason Wheeler

PATIENT: Peetie, a Westie mix dog

DIAGNOSIS: Peetie, a pup, has previously eaten a tube of toothpaste. This time, he gets into the menthol rub. By the time his owner Gary finds him, he has consumed more than half of a large bottle.

TREATMENT: There are a lot of ingredients in the menthol rub, but Dr. Wheeler is most concerned about the ingredient camphor, a poison. After making Peetie vomit, he gives him charcoal to absorb any toxins that are left.

FOLLOW-UP: Peetie will be fine. The bathroom is now definitely off-limits for this playful pup.

Love Thy Neighbor

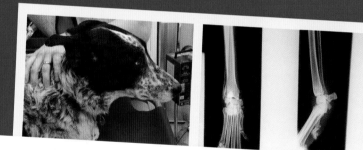

EMERGENCY VETS: Dr. Jeff Steen & Dr. Mark Albrecht

PATIENT: Cassie, a dog

DIAGNOSIS: Betty Jean's dog Cassie ran out of her house and was hit by a car. Betty Jean has an injured hip and couldn't get Cassie to the vet. Neighbors whom Betty Jean doesn't even know helped her get Cassie to Alameda East. "When you have emergencies like this, you have all these wonderful strangers who come in to help you," says Betty Jean.

TREATMENT: Dr. Jeff Steen, Cassie's vet, discovers that her left leg is broken. In spite of this, Cassie's overall health is good.

The next day Dr. Albrecht sets Cassie's leg bone, the ulna, with a bone plate. Unfortunately Cassie also has a sprained right wrist and must have another surgery.

FOLLOW-UP: Cassie spends weeks at the vet hospital while she has these two surgeries. She's home now, and although she is still limping, Betty Jean believes she will soon walk normally again.

Kiva's Stones

EMERGENCY VET: Dr. Holly Knor

PATIENT: Kiva, a dog

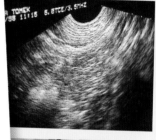

DIAGNOSIS: Will and Jeannie adopted Kiva. She had been with them for three days and had really bonded when they discovered she had little stones in her urine. Without hesitation, they brought Kiva to Alameda. Kiva has been aware of Jeannie's blindness and has stayed at her side. Will hopes that Kiva can be a working dog who will help Jeannie.

TREATMENT: Kiva is crying, and Dr. Knor urges her to hold on. She is concerned that the stones are causing Kiva pain. An ultrasound shows that Kiva's bladder has lots of little stones in it. Although they can be removed surgically, Dr. Knor hopes there is an easier way. She threads a catheter, a narrow tube, into Kiva's bladder and flushes it with fluids. It works. The stones are forced out!

FOLLOW-UP: Kiva will rest for the night and go home with her adoptive parents the next day.

Tree Climbing Dog

EMERGENCY VET:	**Dr. Lauren Prause**
PATIENT:	**Tucker, a cocker spaniel**

DIAGNOSIS: Tucker climbs trees to chase squirrels. His owners Chris and Lisa are making breakfast one morning when suddenly they hear a loud thump. They rush outside to find Tucker has fallen from a tree. This cocker spaniel is crazy about chasing squirrels and has previously fallen from a tree. This time he fell from a greater height. Tucker is having problems breathing so his owners rush him to Alameda.

TREATMENT: Dr. Prause takes X-rays of Tucker. She fears the irregular breathing might be caused by air or fluid trapped in his chest. Fortunately the X-rays are normal, showing that his lungs are clear. Apparently Tucker got the wind knocked out of him!

FOLLOW-UP: Dr. Prause sends Tucker home to rest with advice not to climb any more trees! Chris and Lisa take their wonder dog home and try to keep his feet on the ground.

TUCKER

think you want to be a vet?

Do you love being around animals and taking care of them? Would you be good talking to people about the well-being of their pets and other animals? If the answer to both of these questions is yes, you might want to consider becoming a vet. Keeping animals healthy is an extremely satisfying career.

Becoming a Vet

During high school and college, take lots of science courses, including biology, chemistry, and animal science. Earning good grades is important especially in math and science. After graduating from college, you must attend veterinary school, which is another four-year program.

Like the interns at Alameda East, some new doctors work at internships for one year, followed by a two or three year residency after graduating from vet school. During these internships they put their knowledge to work on animals under the supervision of more experienced vets. They also determine the area of vet medicine they want to pursue as a career.

Basics

Veterinary Medicine

Some vets choose to work with small animals. Others prefer to work with large animals at zoos and circuses or on farms. Still others prefer to work with exotics like reptiles or amphibians. Whichever animals you choose to work with, specialties to consider include zoo animal medicine, radiology, nutrition, surgery, and biotechnology.

Getting Started

You have many years to decide if vet medicine is the right field for you. In the meantime, to find out if you truly love working with and caring for animals, consider:

+ Volunteering at your local vet's office. You'll probably clean cages, but you'll be around animals and will see firsthand many of the things a vet does each day. You'll also learn the responsibilities of a veterinary technician or assistant, another career you could pursue.

+ Volunteering at a local pet store.

+ Volunteering at a zoo, the Humane Society, or an animal rescue organization.

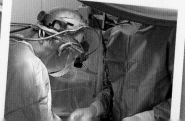

how safe is your house?

Food Dangers

Many foods that people enjoy and keep in their kitchens can be harmful and even deadly if consumed by animals. Never feed the following foods to your pets, even in small amounts:

+ coffee grounds/coffee beans
+ grapes/raisins
+ chocolate
+ onions
+ yeast dough
+ tea
+ macadamia nuts
+ alcohol
+ fatty foods
+ salt
+ avocado
+ garlic
+ chewing gum, candy, and breath fresheners containing xylitol

Do not feed your pets table scraps. Not only are they not good for them, some contain bones that can cut their mouths or cause more serious problems if swallowed.

Cleaning Supply Dangers

Many cleaning supplies can be used safely around the house, but others can be harmful when pets are present. Make sure everyone in the family reads the labels carefully. If they say "keep pets and children away until dry," follow directions! Bleach and other detergents can cause your pets an upset stomach, drooling, vomiting, or diarrhea. If swallowed, they can cause severe burns. To be safe, keep all cleaning products in a cabinet that pets can't get into. Also keep them in their original packaging. This way if your pets accidentally get into them, you'll know exactly what is in the substance.

Medication Dangers

Medicines that make people feel better are often deadly when taken by pets. Keep the following medications in a cabinet your pets can't reach or open:

+ acetaminophen
+ diet pills
+ antihistamines
+ vitamins
+ antidepressants
+ prescription drugs
+ over the counter medicines

Harmful Household Products

+ soap
+ sunblock
+ toothpaste
+ liquid potpourri
+ mothballs*
+ tobacco products
+ pennies
+ alkaline batteries (like those in remote controls)

*Just one mothball can cause serious illness.

Garage and Yard Dangers

Although the garage may seem like a good place to keep a pet while your family is gone for a few hours, think again. A garage is full of toxic substances, including:

+ antifreeze
+ coolants
+ insecticides
+ plant/lawn fertilizers
+ weed killers
+ ice melting products
+ gasoline
+ paint thinners
+ paints

If you plan to keep a pet in the garage, make sure all toxic substances are on a shelf or in a cabinet out of reach.

If your lawn is treated with chemicals, make sure your pets stay off the grass until the chemicals have dried. Otherwise they are likely to swallow some as they lick themselves while cleaning.

+ What to Do If Your Pet Is Poisoned

If your pet is poisoned, alert an adult and call your vet or the Animal Poison Control Center immediately. The faster your pet is treated, the better the chances of making a full recovery. Bring the product container with you to help the vets know what they are treating.

animal behavior tips

CATS

LITTER BOX TIPS Keep the litter box in a place that is convenient and private for your cat. Always keep the litter as clean as possible so your cat will want to use it. If your cat soils outside the litter box, it may have a medical problem. Have a vet examine your cat for any problems, such as urinary tract infections.

HOW TO INTRODUCE A NEW CAT TO OTHER PETS Keep the new cat in a room by itself with a litter box, bed, water, and food. Feed your established pets and new cat on either side of the door to the room the new cat is staying in. Each day move the dishes closer to the door until the pets eat directly across from one other. They will associate the joy of eating with one another's scents. Then open the door enough so the animals can see one another and continue the process.

PET ID TIP Cats and dogs always need to wear a collar with identification and phone number, in case of an emergency.

Switch beds or toys between the animals so they get used to one another's scent.

TEACH YOUR CAT TO SCRATCH ACCEPTABLE OBJECTS Don't punish your cat for scratching. Scratching is normal behavior for a cat. Cats scratch for many reasons, including to mark their territory (they have scent glands in their paws). To keep cats from scratching your rugs and furniture, point them in the direction of acceptable places to claw. Place objects such as rope-wrapped posts near the places they've been scratching. Cover the things you don't want your cat to scratch with items such as double-sided sticky tape, aluminum foil, or a plastic rug cover with the pointy side up. You may even spray scents that cats find unpleasant, such as orange or lemon, on things you don't want your cats to destroy. Keep items covered and continue spraying the scents until your cats are consistently scratching the acceptable objects.

DOGS

HOW TO KEEP YOUR DOG FROM BITING

Dogs can get excited when they are playing, get a little carried away, and bite. Play calmly with your dog. If a dog is biting during play time, you should address this with an adult immediately. Biting behavior should be addressed with the aid of a trainer or animal behavioralist as soon as possible.

Understand that quick movements and loud noises may scare your dog, and it may bite for self-protection. To avoid this, keep the noise level down. Never approach a dog by reaching toward its face or mouth. Do not pull food or toys out of a dog's mouth.

INTRODUCING YOUR NEW DOG TO YOUR OTHER DOGS

Dogs are territorial, so introduce the new dog to your established dog in a place neither one has been. Each dog should be on a leash handled by a separate person. Allow the dogs time to sniff each other for short periods of time, and reward them with treats and encouraging words.

DOGS AND BARKING

It is normal for dogs to bark at times, but too much barking indicates a problem. Make sure you don't leave your dog alone for long periods of time. When you can't be around, provide a comfortable environment with toys.

FERRETS

+ A baby ferret is called a kit.
+ A newborn ferret is so tiny it can fit in a teaspoon.
+ Ferrets have no inborn fear of humans.
+ Ferrets live an average of 6 to 7 years.
+ Sometimes ferrets sleep so soundly it is difficult to wake them.

anim
fac

CATS

+ A cat can smell more than 30 times better than people.
+ A cat's nose has a pattern of ridges that are unique to it (similar to people's fingerprints).
+ There are 33 breeds of cats.
+ Kittens cannot see or hear when they are born. They open their eyes after about five days and develop hearing and sight after about two weeks. Kittens begin to walk when they are about 20 days old.
+ Cats in the wild live about 2 to 3 years. Indoor cats live an average of 15 years.

RABBITS

+ On average, a domestic rabbit lives 8 to 12 years.
+ A happy rabbit will click its teeth.
+ Rabbits will lick and nibble you to show affection.
+ Rabbits are active at night. They spend the day underground.

DOGS

+ Irish wolfhounds are the largest dogs. Chihuahuas are the smallest.
+ Most puppies don't wag their tails until they are about 1 month old.
+ Dogs were among the first animals tamed by people.
+ Dalmatian puppies are born totally white. Their spots appear as they grow.
+ The oldest known dog lived to be 29 years and 5 months old.

glossary

ACUPUNCTURE: an ancient therapy that involves placing small needles in different parts of the body to heal it

ANESTHESIA: a substance used to relieve pain that brings about a loss of sensation

ANTIBIOTIC: a drug that kills or slows the growth of germs

ANTIVENIN: medicine given to stop the effects of a poisonous venom

BIOPSY: a procedure during which a small sample of tissue, cells, or fluids is removed for closer testing

CATHETER: a narrow tube that allows fluids to drain or be injected into a body cavity

CHARCOAL: a substance delivered directly to the stomach that absorbs poisons

DIGESTIVE SYSTEM: the system that breaks down food so it can be used by the body

DOMESTIC: tame; not wild

ENDOSCOPE: a long, thin tube with a camera attached that allows doctors to see inside patients

EPINEPHRINE: a heart stimulant

EXOTIC: not naturally found in a region or country

FEMUR: a bone of the hind leg

INFECTION: virus or bacteria that causes disease or contaminates

PNEUMONIA: a disease in which the lungs become filled with thick fluid and swell

RADIUS: a bone on the inside part of the arm

REIKI: a therapy in which a practitioner uses hands as a focus for healing and giving energy

RINGWORM: a fungus that causes ring-shape patches on the skin

SURGERY: an operation performed to treat a disease, injury, or some other deformity

TUMOR: abnormal growth of cells

X-RAY: a kind of radiation that can pass through the skin to take pictures of the inside of the body